CHRISTIAN NAME
LAWRENCE GIFFIN

UGLY DUCKLING PRESSE
BROOKLYN, NEW YORK
2012

CONTENTS

She entered quickly into a ritual play during which she would eventually destroy the object [....] She would often accompany her own actions with cries of "Stop it"—burst out laughing and repeat the action.

—Dr. James Kent, regarding his patient Susan "Genie" Wiley

*Don't you yet notice
a shimmer on bad zero, won't you walk there
and be the shadow unendurable now calibrated.*

—J.H. Prynne, "Biting the Air"

IN OTHER WORDS IN A THOUGHT IN WHICH
A CONSCIOUSNESS OF FOUNDERING SURVIVES

The Sea
was at my feet.
The Sea.
I too   knew
it was
immense! awful!
I knew the word that
named the process
going on inside my head,
was restrained   The Sea
and made
in fact
herself to point.

My first conscious perception
of an abstract idea. Part I:
Helen's Genius   She touched
my head and said
with decided emphasis,
"The Sea."

I did not know
that words existed.
My ideas were vague
        and my
vocabulary inadequate;
but as I learned
more and more words,
my field of inquiry broadened.

      In this way,
perception posed
a problem for beauty:
that things seen
are temporal   and
things unseen eternal.

For whoever makes some sentence out of
words utters not his wisdom, but
the wisdom of his race
whose life is in the words, though
they had never had such an order
before; instead
thought is presented to
man as language
understanding the very stuff
that language is made of
the thought the experience
of his race, that language must be
one used by a nation, not an artificial thing.

I am also in Arcadia. I secrete
the concealments of god,
masturbate to excess, and covet
many intentional objects Part
                    II: Genie's
Hell in   a lake
where no item is
redeemed
by mouth.   The Sea
goes back and forth on her word.
                    A face painted
in a mirror, a facet pained
by letters, those obliterated
by facility   and skirted
by capitals, by curious men.
Every corpse describes
          the orifice it
was intended to conceal,
one that opens onto
the world   and   contents.
In this way,   haecceitas
presents itself   on
the outskirts   of the city.

Void of thought,
always falling   suddenly and
                    suddenly,
the mind I have learned and
the thing I have been drop
away without dreaming.
          All the light and music.
    In a room, there never was
an object that spoke
and did not disappear.
A timeline flattened against
the far wall.
There may come a time
when people   will never
need to have been.
All the light and music.

The sun is   a lazy Susan.
The Sea, taking   everything,
admits nothing,
and pounding, registers
its gifts in self-effacement,
and contemplating
the source of its outpouring,
one enters its   comings
and goings under the identity
of opposites,   of a rule
eliminated in application.
Yet, the mysteries leading thought
to mysticism
find their solution
in human
practice,   in the
politics of this practice.
All the light and music.
In this way,
collectivity constitutes
a contradiction for
consciousness.

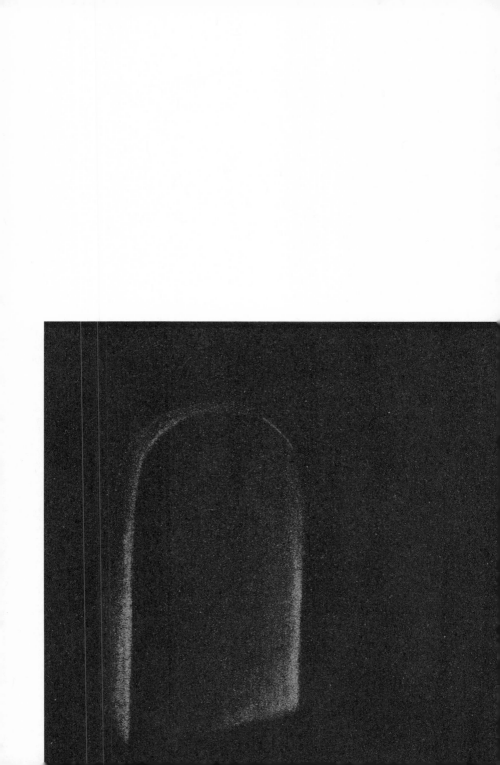

PRESQUE VU

A brown dawn fluctuates
      along foundation
            and misconduct.
The moon is overtaken
      in its concealment
            and cycles down
into contrivances.

The dream of architecture,
      which eclipsed
            the violence of its
inception, collapsed
      the volition of its
            inaner epic in a wake
founding the circumference
      of her pink city-state.

One recites only excerpts
      from a tentative redaction
            of some apocrypha
reconstructed after the fact
      that one happens to be,
            happens upon this

originary hut through
      the negation of abandon.

Still, lacking
      the word will not
            star her consequence.
Tomorrow will be just
      a misworded account
            declaimed from memory.

A CHILDISH PASSION FOR BALLS

A paternity of snowfall calmed us,
and your young thoughts turned to love
and the touch of lips so sweet.
Addulced. Some have called thee,
"MILF for all seasons."

Your thoughts turned to low clouds.
They are meat agape. And sprechen veritas.
They are wheelchair effervescence in
orthopedic declension,
hands across my America
that have a little tea service.

Your young thoughts accost us
because they are fig.-less
not because fabric softener fathered,
in the creases of empurpled Oprah guests,
a proper name. Rubber balls and liquor.

IN LOCO PARENTIS

1.

May we no longer with license be
    but with lice aplenty mete
        yr bacchantic hysterics
            in apollonian Babyface,

first secreted then secreted
    as a sumptuous *semper fidelis*
        that rations libertinage as *Rights of Man*?

Could we not appeal to
    the wild side of this
        daughter to a wolf whistler's
            will to womanpower?

A little earthen puissance, maybe,
    camped out *in flagrante delicto*.
A garden inferred from an untyped
    token, tesseract cast
        as tessera tied to a training pot
            to end up a test market for *Teletubbies*.

You are our happy Eden, our ending,
    the crowd's roar at *Flughafen Nürnberg*
        registered by the primitive recording
            equipment of the day as *Eine Kleine*
    Kristallnachtmusik, tiny terror
        of being there without having to go.

2.

The accretion disk of history,
    composing its perspective effect,
        turns round a too-soon
            interregnum only
    to mistake that thought for
        the transpiration of utopia,
    not to recognize that each thought
        is a door that leads one only away.

What remains: period piece, daily life.
    How its content contains unrestrained
        as shifted fetishes persist in reversing
        the flow of intention outward
from things without measure or making.

    City of detours
        where she has not an obstructed
        memorial of dispensation.

The prize of us, object that consents
　　to production. What you wore, waste
　　　　management. The consent that objects
　　　　　　to usufruct. Still mute so to speak.

Still, mute, which is not to say patient,
　　waiting to the extent that we could define
　　　　ourselves *in loco parentis*, in absence
　　　　　　of a bounty against opportunity.

She does not fascinate because
　　she affords us an expletive as Idea,
　　　　transposing in the sense of severance
　　　　　　as in of an estate or limb.

JOKES AND THEIR RELATION TO
THE UNCONSCIOUS

You exude non-participation in a simultaneous bedroom
with its scant organs advanced upon the carpet in trust.
You just push off into the catastrophe unequal to itself,
padding its trench-wear with the prognosis of allelic calligraphy.

Ms. Meredith, has your child yet composed
            his *Kindertotenlieder*?
Or, has he collapsed into a shadow of transaction,
threshold whence thinking returns
to the mechanical wunderkind unharmed.

Funny, I was just thinking.

Held up, a felt and unethical jewel
infinitesimally within this word
that bears you crosswise
to the procession of people becoming people.

Waves lick the child's rigidity—green and oceanic.
They touch you in your sleep, your young interval
and leave it at that with nothing left to say.

THE PLAYTHING OF MY THOUGHT

In the highly developed organisms the receptive cortical layer
has long been withdrawn into the depths of the interior of the body,
though portions of it have been left behind on the surface
immediately beneath the general shield set up against stimuli.

These are the sense organs, which consist essentially
of the apparatus for the reception of certain and diverse effects
of stimulation, but which also include special arrangements
for further protection against unsuitable kinds of stimuli.

> Example 1: Leaving your child in a room by herself.
> Your child needs to learn to cope with your absence.
> Don't reason with the little gal. Discipline her.
>
> The unpleasureable nature of an experience doesn't
> always unsuit it for play.
>
> For this task, parents would be wise to keep a large
> repertoire of disciplinary strategies in their hats.

When the rules change and when the punishment becomes
capricious, if she can withstand and not buckle, if it doesn't hurt,
then she must walk a few feet into a slightly darkened room
while Mother counts to ten. She knows she can come out
if she wishes. The length of time in the dark is lengthened,
and, instead of producing fear, it produces stars
and eventually a CD player—a source of pleasure for a small child.

We see how the germ of a living animal recapitulates the structures of all the forms from which it is sprung, instead of proceeding quickly by the shortest path to its final shape.

In this instance, where the child proceeds from the passivity of the experience to the activity of the game, there is a yield of pleasure from another source.

Of course, the child's sexual researches ultimately lead to no satisfactory conclusions, yet for the last one hundred and fifty years, the Western world has viewed childhood in a positive light, as one of the happiest phases of a person's existence.

It is only consistent to grant that there was a time before the purpose of childhood was the fulfillment of wishes.

> Example 2: Tableau vivant.
> Susan giggles as she waits for her date to come around and open the car door. The pair enters an ice cream shop. She sits down at the table as her date gently pushes in her chair. He takes her hand from across the table and asks, "What flavor would you like tonight, Sugar?" Susan smiles and says, "I'll have chocolate, Daddy."

If he flat-out rejects her, she will replace him.
If he is warm and nurturing, she will look for a lover to equal him.

If he thinks she is beautiful, worthy, and feminine, she will be inclined—
she whom her father loves so well.

More and more fathers are becoming aware of their influence
and regularly dating their daughters.

"I have tremendously more impact on my daughter than my wife does.
Right now I have an opportunity to love her or reject her."

THE PROMISED UNITY OF DESIRE AND ITS OBJECT: A POEM TO SUSAN WILEY

You get nothing. A bubble that climbs
from the bottom of the glass, breaks
on the surface inaudibly. This is
the thanks we get, and none expected.

Is it horror, immediacy? Yet it all is
still functioning. Isn't everything
in its own way? Could it be,
a world that misses nothing?

It is possible you are longer still
in your faculties, your facility, where
a training film obscures the blackboard.
Your logic copied in an ooze of half-masticated food,

your universal quantifier improvised
in the wake you leave in anything,
inverted yes, but wandering freely
in your mincing gait. It's not

that we can't effect your status,
it's that we can't yet because
we do now, because registration staves off
the fanciful nearness of distant extinction.

You are a symbol because we can't
quite get a hold of you. But then again,
you are not for us, are you?
Perhaps, in that way, you are more our
future than our past. The mute inhuman

waiting to be born amidst the implants
and neural jacks of a world so humanized
as to no longer offer any ground
against which to conceive the human.

AN ILLUSION OF THE FUTURE

What would her boy's fate be? she wondered. Well, she decided,
they need a victim. I need a victim. We all need a victim.

—Diane Williams

Pilgrimage   Their son chose
when He would
wean Himself

the second Sunday
of the month
was Mother's Day

lavender walls and
a large picture window
a cluster of outbuildings
a barn a
house
a building a
hut

in this
part of Nebraska

Forty-two His father's family
Generations had had the land
from David for generations
to Christ

maternal forebears
two failed marriages
Six months later
a dozen years earlier

raising greyhounds
and selling them to racetracks

moved out and married
young

Shroud of a child's pose
Turin handsome and gangly
small and fair-skinned, with
a Friesian mane of hair
eyes filled with tears

the afternoon
on Mother's Day
making jewelry,

lifting weights,
baking cheesecake,

rough-cut stone
difficult but enchanting

Prophecies   every generation of children is more
Concerning   academically and environmentally
the Messiah   advanced than the previous generation

and then
there are the rare few who are really
superstars among the stars
"it's hard to argue that those superstars
don't exist."

Annunciation   Even before He was born,
His Mother wanted a boy
His Mother had definite ideas
about her child

she later described the moment in
a letter to her future husband,

His Father had a vasectomy as soon
as she gave birth—
"I decided to grow up then and there,
solemnly renouncing the rest of childhood"

*The Virgin
and Child
Enthroned and
Surrounded by
Angels*

He clamored vigorously
for His mother's attention
while she was doing
some bookkeeping
My mom and I
all-we-need-is-each-other

*The Finding
in the Temple*

He questions authority on a reg-
ular basis and is quick to pick up on how
serious the situation is and how far he
can push. He doesn't like to be asked
questions. He often responds with "Why
don't I ask you a question?"

Herod's Reign

case studies of these children,
vast accumulations of detail pertaining
to family histories, head circumferences,

grip measurements, and prepubescent doodles
public schools as a "form of discrimination
that makes me think of Nazi Germany"

John the
Baptist

an eight-year-old boy
threatened suicide and
was later found to have been
heavily coached on the text
by his mother, who had obtained
a copy in advance

the boy suffered from a culture
that treats extremely bright children as freaks

It's the gifted kids who are beaten up
It's not safe to be gifted

Childhood

"We had always considered homeschooling
something for religious freaks, and both of us
were hard-core anti–organized religion"

they decided to save money by skipping grades
five through eight and going straight to the high-
school curriculum

"We never pushed Him

"All of His motivation came from within

"He got to see birth, death, to see the seasons
in their entirety"

Ministry   For the next three years,
       He traveled across Nebraska

       His talent was more on the
       emotional, spiritual side

The Gospels someone
       might "write a little biographical book
       and look back at when He was fourteen
       and see that this was when He was
       learning the groundwork for what
       was going to make Him famous
       when He was in His twenties and thirties"

Hypostasis "To have the intelligence
       of an adult and the emotions

of a child combined in a childish
body is to encounter certain difficulties"

some people think that their rate
of suicide may be higher than average.
Among the factors cited, besides the risks
of social and intellectual isolation, are
the attendant pressures of perfectionism
(described by one psychologist as "an
emotional need to develop themselves and
master the world")

"It's an ability to make connections
between all kinds of things and sense
meaning in the abstract; everything mat-
ters to them, all the animals He'll encounter
underground, and all the children"

"A lot of gifted kids are angels
who are on this earth with
responsibilities to help others"

trapped in a nine-year-old's body

"There's no other way to explain it"

The Two　　　"All the girls were madly
Marys　　　in love with Him,

　　　His suicide rocked
　　　their world." She
　　　smiled a
　　　wistful smile

The Virgin　　　"I went all the way through high
　　　school without doing the girlfriend
　　　thing. The temporary girlfriend—
　　　what a waste of time"

Teachings and　　　It's
Parables　　　like water, basically. It doesn't
　　　require tremendous technique.
　　　He said, "I'll take you on,
　　　but you're going to learn
　　　how to ease people's pain"

　　　He said, "Basically, O.K.,
　　　there's this living stuff
　　　and we call it organisms."
　　　He found it incredibly abstract

New Age–style washes of chords
and arpeggios, entitled "Elements"

Via Crucis   Christmas

His mother had taken him to
the library in Ogallala, where
she was signing copies of her
latest novel, "Victim Wanted."
"IT'S HER FAULT I WAS
BORED OUT OF MY MIND."

Crucifixion   Christmas

seeing the snow falling upward

He chose when He
would wean Himself

She ran upstairs
and saw His body
crumpled on the floor.

La Pietà His father carried Him in his arms
to the car, called **911**, and began
driving Him toward town

Deposition and The harvesting of His organs took place
Entombment over the next two and a half days.
Despite extensive damage to His brain,
the rest of His body was functioning.
They said they were fortunate to
get a body in such good shape

Descent into She had contacts with Him
Hell after He'd left His body.
Then there was none for
forty-eight hours. But then
they both felt a sense of peacefulness.
And He took the memory away

Resurrection His heart is now beating
and Ascension in the chest of an **11**-year-old boy.
I am trembling and crying as I write this,
but I want to share with you
and the rest of the world that knows Him

Christology   She became taken with the idea that
perhaps He'd actually killed Himself so
that His organs could be put to use
in those who needed them

"I'm ambivalent about Christianity,
but a lot of people have said He
reminded them of Jesus. You know:
'He came, He taught, He left.'"

She believed that He was spiritually gifted,
and that His mission to assist others in this
lifetime may have been fulfilled by His death

He had a kind of
ancient wisdom
that was beyond anybody

A more intelligent kid
can sense his mother's bad mood
with less data,
and a child who sees more is more
likely to experience anxiety himself
when his mother is anxious

"He was so spiritually aware that
if He sensed that people needed
His help He would have helped"

"I asked Him for guidance, because
I could have missed something."
And when she woke up the next
morning, she said, "I had this over-
whelming sense of peace, and just
the feeling that He'd gone home."

"Well, I can tell you what the spirits
are saying: He was an angel."

"He was an angel who came down to
experience the physical realm for a
short period of time."

"He's become a teacher. He says
right now He's actually being taught
how to help these people who
experience suicides for much messier
reasons. Before He was born, this was
planned. And He did it the way he did
so that others would have use of his body.
Everything worked out in the end."

The Day of Pentecost	At the very least, the suicide appeared now to be something they had the vocabulary to understand

The Church Militant	One afternoon the sky darkened

"I see moms who smoked
all through gestation, or moms
who yell at their kids at the store,
and I look at the kids and they're so
beaten down."

His father had taught him
construction. Over a single
weekend, He learned
woodworking

This memory
remained

"He changed all the rules.
It was the first year we had
a real lawn."

NOTHER

Your poor copy bears
a Satanic heading;

its body, a sieve
that holds back the final word
on what will have
become

your preferred
form of address.

Masterful.

A minimum of speech,
whatever, abutting horror,
perfection of everydayness.

Nother remains but i.e.,

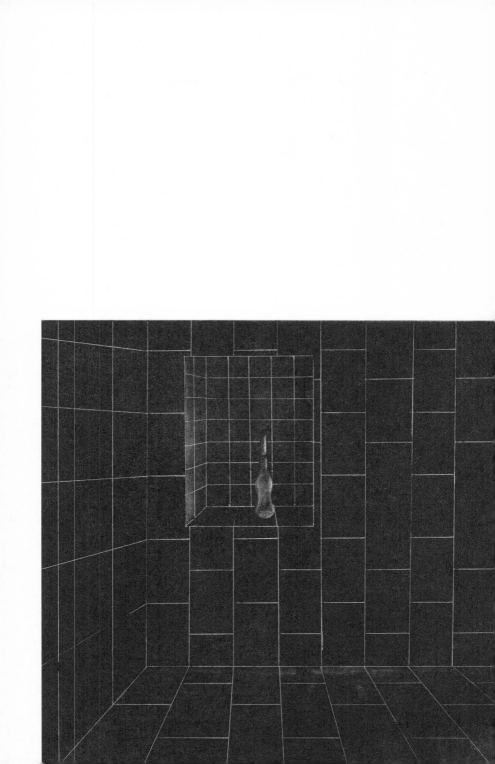

THE LIBERATION

First you tossed the ring
that bound you to your double,
along with a destiny
slyly tethered to your homeland.
Now you can't sit still,
and hours no longer
turn into days, weeks,
to stand for the troubled erection of
this artifice that makes a master of you.

I was surprised not so much
by Stockhausen's comment
as by the fact that he was
still living. It's something
you would like to have said
yourself, somewhere you
would like to have traveled.
Instead, you laze on the couch.

It is summer. It is winter.

It reads like something I
picked up at such-and-such
academy for girls, such that

just being stupid
gives one the impression
of having forgotten something
worth remembering: depictions of violence
bound for the surface of things
whose affect is afforded by guesswork,
as a terror that lingers
in place of the beautiful doll,
the fuzzy animalcule, alone
in the backyard.

Rather, imagine
a disengaged latch
instead of the memory
of what it was like to be me then.
Like a cathedral where no cathedral
stood. It was a sculpture, now
it is a monument to our solvency
only in death, to wringing more out
of exported deficit and wingéd outfitting.

My fear is that time
will heal the wounds
before I have had my chance
to finger them.

And still, this possessiveness remains intact,
and bends until the word becomes bird,
flower, cloud. Something sticky,
a clump of hair, some
handwriting I still do not
recognize as such
in the terrific and accidental destiny
of having to be always an animal
die-cast in specificity.

It is summer. It is winter.
You laugh, but the wind
carries it away.

THE BELLMAKER'S ORPHAN

The cathedral, the caveat that
uttered and unvoiced persists,
insists in your insouciance.
But your thought is a
decontextualized
murderball of just having to be:
"I am just here. I just am here."

Just there, across
the omnipresence of imaginary terror,
a means not so much
to actual terror
but to mark terror's
aimless autonomy—
a way to keep it close.

By the time these words reach you,
you will have other names for those people,
those thoughts. Those who want for nothing. First
no better than the last. This land
no farther from empty fields after plague, its city
begrudgingly replenished with pagans.

But the pagan is only a means, as is
his paganism, which now thrown under
the logic of a monopolized transcendental
is the city that sets us in motion,
occupying spaces settled
in a momentum without monument.

It wants you to indicate your category
of lived experience
in the pharmaceutical brochure.

It is still so difficult to answer
for the future; the future
takes forever.
But I think you can see
how you came to take my place
in the imperative light of confessions made
not to delay bodily pain but out
of an unresponsive tickle
that just happens to be.
Black beam flashing from cursorial
to cursory, returning by another route
to choke the user on its cursive graffiti.

PERFECT RECALL

Like our neighbor's patio furniture,
dumped on our lawn by heavy winds,
I find the contents of my thought unfamiliar
and the boy all grown up.

What's the matter? Did your mommy
not love you enough for it to stop hurting?
Guess what. She didn't.

She wrote poetry. She wrote hate mail,
that is, she hated the fact that a second
book of political philosophy would be
put out before she had finished the first one.

An entire housing project will be erected
against this. Over its towers, the sun
will peak and reveal the vague mass
in the driveway to be the hacked-up remains
of the ping-pong table our neighbors stored for us.

For holiday shopping. For uninhabitable vacation.
Go into the lite. Go into the diet Panzer
pressed against a weird pit, a pocked reminiscence.

When we touch wine coolers, the clinking
punctuates your rhythm as you exercycle
your way through May, June, July. Irrevocable,

yet safe we go.
Returning from a weekend at the Cape, the Keys,
the lake, the colonies.

The coulter from an old plow nailed
to the restaurant's wall. Colorful representation
of peasants in the duke's book of hours. Poor
shepherds who only now discover death
comes also for them. Nature is their Louvre;
and hard times, their Sorbonne. Someone
somewhere sees the bird I want
to write about and stupidly smiles.

ENCHANTED WHATEVER

In averting one's gaze, it comes to rest
elsewhere, on something now scored
or scoured with coincidence.

This is exactly what is not meant
by meaninglessness, by the loss
of meaning, the loss of a cellphone.

Rather, in the last place I look,
which meaning essentially is,
a gesture appears with no end in sight.

A rusted sign retains its
imperative washed out in
a relapse that is abruptly prophetic,
each frustrated desire for contingency now
hollow, bleached, chill—
an edifice that dons this life like flayed skin.

This is exactly what is not meant by advertising.

And the model, lit
across watery contexts,
is what we reach for; as in,

we reach for her in her place.
What she reaches for is us.

And the hand that takes us by the hand
is our hand gloved—placed
in a glove-shaped hand.

She says, "desire objects," not in the sense
of an objective. An object. I mean,
product. I mean, what it isn't.

That is exactly what is not meant
by a telephone that squirts shit
into your mouth, hoarse truth.

The images are airbrushed
into blur, as if
captured in retreat, but really it is only
our shameful projection of falling away.

At the pinnacle of its perfection,
the body only lapses in recounting.
The body that sees and hears,
that beautifully thinks such thoughts as praxis.

Great, but now what?

ATAVISTA

This is not my shit.
                  This is not my play
list. This is not the Monday morning
                  of the body of Christ
exiting my inner adventure play
          that isn't yet a passion play.

          This is the perceived
          dependency threatened
          by external influences. It is called
          end-user. It is called
          carceral parent model. Suspect,

          see how it looks on you,
how it pains you to reveille in our painted sky,
the "I spy" of some blue ideals
          under which we are led
                  further afield,
          under whose gaze we stay
                  the straight
          severity, the white ray,
          saccular and seamed (an
             unseemly
                air of contrariety).

Silver planet
only
of eve and morn,

of tear and tear,
        find and replace.

To see "it"
mirror'd small in a paradise. *In antis*,
taking a chance on a lot to take in
and so depose the day so detached
that you conceal with the sky
all agnostic prospects.
        To let oneself be not one who
discerns what reveals but leaves
it to them otherfucking eyes
behind God's lights to stray the State
verity the right way, the Tao
and change, *The Unfinished
System of Nonknowledge*, Revised
Edition, trans. by YouTube.com
into a crappy lo-res version
of DOS capital-*T* truth and desk
copy "Justice" for RUN PROGRAM.

You could not have excerpted the continuum.
The chalice only litters the Sea.

You fall for all conveyances
of Civil Power
that satisfy conditions.
Vacuum-fold, Windows98.

        The world as it is actually mistaken.
        The lamb as it is actually severed.
ARE YOU IN TEE *totum pro parte*, a wuttuhl pwaytang? A little
       too much to drink, *peut-être*?
                       Aye,

        remove yourself. Nay, draw nigh.

righting the false mirror to re
dress water
en French,

or to draw in a bath the foundations for
the production of LENIN's TACO
as a reference for autonomic hole in *nulle*
part or words in another social contract.

64

WE LAID IT DOWN. WE GOT TIRED.

Not more or less deprived
of ground given regardlessly
by a syphilitic's tube of concealer,
I still have my likes, my dislikes,
caryatids of fecal columns
grown thin and winded
with righteous authority,
that is, by my need for speech. You see,
I too am pressed by a meeker plume,
piqued by interim and hyphenated,
filched thin by great and little
domesday. I too am sideswiped
by hindsight's blind spot, sickened
by the taint below Love Canal,
by pained and rowdy defenestrators—
and yet, still dying to be
squarely set within inevitability.

Because we flavored this drunken
tizzy with hinged anticipation,
the rest of it gnaws my no. 2
as parous pulp passes into verdure
influence. A child's hide tanned a tawny mess,

popping out that polished penny
dangling before you on a shoestring,
keeping your ass on the line. Brackish wards
washed by flood of new year's shake-
junt beheading, penning itself
in oar-distorted crag's reflexion,
during school-time. Too much
time and else on our hands,
nights not indexed by lines of tread
and tracer fire, too much read into to tell
and like in dreams forced to watch,
to plot the protein shake
in boring parenthetical the breadth
of a troglodyte's selfish trill.

Not just to our word is clapped
the damaged kindness that I held
slack enough to cover my ass,
but also to you, my punitive stipple,
because your waste is small
and your curves picket
my self-abuse of history.
Because you fabled your broach
with bleary lips, because
I had been drinking, because
a protein loosened diagonal

to as many synapses
as bored my stoned sport.
I was beset, besotted
in a land without scapegoat,
in a family plot plopped
with the feral coinage unslotted.

Shame is the one sign of our correct practice.
They speak of it incessantly, now
that it is no longer obvious.
True love lies in eternal ad hoc,
in pierced troth, in fuck all.
Humiliated by some catholic
humanitas, repulsed by some
protestant Naturalismus,
we laid it down; we got tired,
having still to be within range
of necessity, kept restless in a timeliness
suspended in nixing imagination,
even secured in that propaganda,
the future, indistinguishable
from extortion, from that first philosophy,
which makes stuff mine at all and is
clotted by its jot, is copied word
for word onto itself in correction fluid.

PROSTHETIC A PRIORI

No one will remember that you
gestured to the spirit of crime
in war, seduction that first seemed
banal to us in the homeland,
in that, what did we expect?
All the sudden, it had always
been enough—to walk away and
not look back.
                    If only I could
be ashamed and reconstructed
as a list of bad decisions
ending in a show of good faith,
soundless outdoor blunt of tactics,
then I could be broke and mended.
I could be a faceless mass's
point of contact well beyond the
limits of my term in office
and still not stand not in the way
but in for justice as only
you can, with leash in hand.

This history does not judge harshly.
It will not throw the book at you.
Nor abscond the bailiff's kindness

taking you to see its barber,
Necessary Jobbery, which fairs
"laisser les bons tons rouler"
as well as stand-ins for the poorly
recompensed.
           You are not guilty,
any more than you are truly
yours. As judge, not harsh enough,
that is, such requirements as
ours are thus recalled enough to
slap the bloody donut from its fist.
But not shameless me and my one
built-in joy: the given's Christian
name, Necessity.
           To live with
your desire has been difficult,
bears the brunt of another's. But
burden is anything but work.

Occupation is not belonging
even though you stand there or
in spite of the fact.
           History
will not judge harshly or at all;
it will not let you take it off.

WHAT IS AND WHAT IS TO BE DONE

As it abstains, its work becomes just
work; its absence
leaves no vacuum;
its falsity, no truth.

Its hole holds though no longer legible;
its ledger's leaves untotaled,
gathered and burned at dusk.

Distinguished mark
extinguished in light, a right
relinquished to have as ours
our daily bread,

as it is, it is ours
to see to on earth,
wherewithal but without will,
left to want what we are without,
without the word for it.

Word that is not read the same way twice,
rewritten on the far side of its spelling,
not waiting, wanting

not to have to want
to work against one's will,
against want. Despair,

which only can arouse its desire
for that name now misspelled,
can continue, can call forth prescriptions,
compose a sentence wherein the word
can cross its contention already
reconciled unconsciously,
in origins of what aught ought to be.

THE OTHER TASK

In a round word, we return
what we didn't know once
belonged to us
to the scene of the crime
so as to commit it.   We thought
                                  we knew
how to spell its one name,
to pick it out from a lineup,
to get as close as possible without
succumbing to inanity, so near as
to be carried across forgetting
what the word is and how it
makes the body speak
for it in its name
and names it.

The not-the-same-as-once-was, some
antique from that side of its aid
that operates on the fact
that it cannot do what it does to what does it.
Smoked impotence hung at the center of town
to convince you of something
of some worth or to put
that ha'penny paid out back in and in reverse.

They cannot go there with you, nor
do they anticipate a return.
The self-heal of the field,
gold-plated mean. An artist's
interpretation of wildflowers
swapped against
the irredeemable particulate.

                              A wish
to have nothing more to say expressed,
in a word, in a wordless stare,
bovine and turned away.

THE WORLD UPSIDE DOWN

How the Idea is thought in this life
is the parotic estoppel given
to the monolith rising at
the center of its attendant fanfare,
        as well as to the promise of
          its listing decomp
          that its thought at once unthinks,
dispensing the terms it finds just stuffed
in it, like the entrails of some
thing to be divided
piecemeal among the species,
        one day to be
          regarded as total work
          consented to from without.

Form in flames on the bay,
a tenor drops off,
        and where the thread
        is taken up again is
        its blindness
a posture relative to loss
that does not come round again
        or leave its trace
        as warning written

with discarded bits
pulled apart by shear and
torque of intimacy's involution.

A handful cycle back into an
order that appears to repeat
the living word in its triumphant xenolalia,
        abutting the course thought abandoned;
        cuz when they say,
        "You can't take it with you,"
they are curiously convinced,
in that, that is how a tongue
decomposed in apostrophe
lashes out against truth
        only to become aware of some
        drone shadowing neighborliness
        and only in that acreage which
        requires inconstant maintenance.

THE POSSIBLE DREAM

That things would be as they are,
left to the technical parlance of
their profiles and
devoid of motivation.
A monstrosity yet unclaimed
in the unbought contentments
is still serviced by an idea whose
domain is described
by a blast radius.

Dreams are perfect—it's illogical
to think there could be mistakes
anywhere in them.
Nothing intended,
not unless you could say
the psyche itself
is a mistake.

Who then are we to interrupt
the historical task of equipment
that reads and writes the face of the earth
as if it were portended in a dream
and not brought about thereby?

To sleep through their automated thirst,
which springs from us as
from a wound,
no longer dreaming
but shutting one's eyes against it,
unwilling and therefore unable
to see that it is its own dusk
hurled into the defile
through which each is in turn
processed. Much pleasure, then
from these, much more must flow.

PERDURABLE (BEGINNING WITH A LINE FROM PASCAL)

Hither side the Pyrenees are truths,
    which are falsehoods on the other
so that to travel far is to be
    representative abroad of
your flag's stock of docile bodies
    slick with capital and therefore
frictionless, that is, statistical,
    without arms, nevertheless
with digits, whose access is offset
    by increasing constraints at home.

Detained without a proper contra-
    diction in recessive drafting,
constituted by some other
    means, preemptive static. Setting
of history in its selfsame casting,
    out of sync from equal starting.
When you wake up to face the world, it
    comes to you whole, then whole cloth, but
it never becomes a choice you make.
    Every day is like the first day.

That it is always better to be-
    lieve, to be left alone, to pay

for hope in the life that is to come,
    and with the given no less,
is a statistically sure thing.
    A security against you,
against a done deed that is forgot
    yet to be recalled, just as
a path across will only become
    clear with the first paving stone.

THE SUNKEN CATHEDRAL

Water without purpose
now wets with rising tide
the tips of spires
that penetrate a gray sky
not hung with a white cloud
as hundreds of well-dressed
strangers surface with orders
in the master's hand
demanding a regicide come
forth for he cannot
become one himself.

Rains replace the dome's
column of sunlight
and a red night withdraws
as if from a lover
whose now-green lips part
like floodgates in a song
in a voice that strains to
descend into moan
echoing in pink shells
the crest and collision
of faceless swells.

Downriver we wind,
faced down by wind
and songs in it, bells
that break the placid air
with salt and spray,
a sea we stagger into
en masse with a wax phallus
in each ear to pour wine
on the fuck of it, which
diluted, floats away red
like dawn into blue like day.

Drink up and drink down
the blood and piss it out
into the streets, squat low
and fill the gutters face down
until the city drowns
so that its sunken sister rises,
its spires dissolved along with
the cocky saint who got us to
beget without fucking
according to maxims
willed to universal laws.

To that devil, daughter and slave,
whose massacre braids
the nooses that knot this
edifice of dry cobwebs
mounted on misrecognition,
slipping into worship of hap-
piness, we drink, we don't forget
because we read against the grain
of dear souvenirs, which
are just preludes. To what?
Same justice, same beauty.

No more in need
of father's key
or mother's crown,
which come to rest
here with us in
abandon not ablation,
as much remnants
as we are, left
behind to work for
nothing at all, for the promise
of no more tomorrow.

MEGACHURCH

The thing about truth,
a broken guitar,
is that you have to
come away from it.

It has no content
nor any contentment
in the eternal
though ahistoric.

Its strings do not play
recognizable
notes, though it does play,
because truth broke it.

It's stupid not to
want to supercede
the given but want
electric guitars.

Electric guitars
don't break the same way,
and they can be fixed
by guitar repairmen.

The thing about truth,
a broken guitar,
is that it plays you,
because you are broke.

THE ORGAN OF PROJECTION

In just denoted tone
one makes use of it as best one can,
verified by equipment and
by that with which one works.

As if suddenly remembered,
a foretaste from that side of
the pulse of beating rank.

As if from nowhere and untimely,
the unforeseeable cipher
in the noncoincidence of one

pitch. Sublime distraction from
shuffled pages and winded bellows—
crystal buttresses in bad faith
sited thru glorious entry point.

Pizzicati, water drops, tearing silk;
sovereign, proletariat, subject.
A mixture of human and celestial voice.

There's no trick to it, just to be.
What is is not to be done;
tertium non datur.

PRACTICED RESTRAINT

Why write an entire novel
to illustrate the falseness
of human dignity?
We are for repression
and support its work,
the source of all work.

I forget because I haven't
been sentient so long.
I forget because I was
exposed to chemicals as a young lady.
I forget, did he say *du jour* or *de jure*?
Poisson or *poison*? Jesus Christ
or Socrates?
Girls or boys? Nothing at all
or anything at all?

      Sing: *We are stardust. We are golden.*

      ‡

Find a Christmas future and put it in the past,
so when we have a moment, that is,
when you cut your hand and I hold it,
it will take the form of mastery.

You see, when you cut yourself on the machine,
I become a master.

And this is sexual.

"Consented,—and held out"

Sing: *There is a reason. Turn. Turn. Turn.*

‡

Little is lost
on the equipment;
if anything, stuff is
appended to the end
of a tree-lined street,

either a sunken cathedral
or mounted basilica.
The poor or their lack of capital.

And it can be yours, absolutely
free, funded from the busty trebuchet,
burned into the inadmissible thoughts
of people looking up from their work.

It comes into view
as they cross the wide and new
boulevard, and it
continues to loom in their minds as they make
for the shade of some side street—

it doesn't matter which; all empty back

into the main
thoroughfares,
eventually.

Sing: *And so castles made of sand.*

‡

You look askance at the chasm
opening up in the center of town.

You are reminded of something now
so far away that you have become tired,
and you had better go.

Your singular pursuits assuage
your guilt as a prelude only
to the ignorance that slowly

but surely materializes as a
dank jacket of devotion in lieu of practical reason,
a pagan glee that hyphens don't suppress
so much as maintain as *mein* hitch-point
through the long unification.

Sing: *Stopped into a church I passed along the way.*

‡

Some are snug and genuflecting
in the passenger's confidence.
Some are washed out in flaccid and
heartless performance, not that I
thought it wouldn't have been
difficult to reground the more obscure
passages by letting you speak
with the manager, except that
a city just sort of appeared
there as its own understanding
to handle its grief-stricken members.

Remember, Margareta,
when we were so blond?
So young and so small

and so close to the earth that the spirit
just moved right through us?

Sing: *And it's just a box of rain. I don't know who put it there.*

‡

Gone away are the days
when I wanted to taste
the rainbow without
having first to be told to.

Come to stay is the unrecognizable
lack of pubic hair in place of
a twirling grimace that seemed to say,
"This is what crying
on the inside looks like."

And it's that four-lettered
excluded middle in that catch-all,
"love, peace, and harmony,"
that undressed you then and
will now only advance us
unavoidably into pornography.

Sing: *We built this city on rock and roll.*

‡

Fondled by necessity, Etruscan slaves
are just too far behind to take stock
of what about it has changed since we
started putting the whole thing into words.

Houses were fashioned into the tips of spires
reverse engineered from siege machines,
and a new way of thinking brought a sense
of dignity to the controlled implosion of the poor.

What does this retracing actually depict?
Antinomous Islam in outmoded Christendom.
There should be nothing to let happen. My own
private public horizon. My own intermittent slough.

My other god's an atheist, a.k.a. Cloaca Maxima,
whose back is turned to us. We believe in it
as long as it remains in the dark, and that
is our great excuse for not knowing any better.

Sing: *Shine on you crazy diamond.*

EASE OF MOBILITY

      Afterwards, when one
would have said as much: some sort
of bloody fortitude—
Geschichte in verse,
internment, catastrophe.
It is summer. It is winter.

                A bit of the world
got in my mouth. It felt cool the first time,

as a child, tumbling
into the misconstrued present.
Forced to make do
when the right is primed. It is summer.

It is winter.
A smattering of days falls to the side;
they no longer seem the indices
that living them promised.

Today is a gift. You
know how you can tell?
It's got your name written on it
in your handwriting. It reads, "Equipment."

NOMEN OBLITUM (SOME EXTRACTS AND ADDITIONS)

You are a person of some interest
That might prove useful and yet never proves
Or finds [her] hour [tied
to a potty chair, bound in
a sleeping bag and placed in a crib].

*The cradle rocks above two eternities of darkness. Although they are
identical, man, as a rule, views the prenatal abyss with more calm
than the one he is heading for.*

*Children and ghosts, as unstable signifiers, represent the disconti-
nuity and difference between the two worlds.*

[Something other than duration.]
   patient, I have seen you sit
Hours to verify [...], inform curiosity [...], carry report.

[A voice not unlike your own]
   is itself movement.
Unable to speak a word,
Swaddled in darkness. In the
[putrescence of the potty chair].

And now good morrow to our waking soules,
Which watch not one another out of feare;
For love, all love of other sights controules,
And makes one little roome

*[a] room that resembles a reverie, a truly spiritual room, where the
stagnant atmosphere is lightly tinged with pink and blue.*

*Poets send out the sick spirit to green pastures [....] A sort of
yarb-doctors in their way, poets have it that for sore hearts, as for
sore lungs, nature is the grand cure. But who [...] made an idiot
of Peter the Wild Boy?*

[...] the innate depravity of man's nature [...]
[from which will follow forever
and a day, as if written on
his wooden rod and only now recalled].

*The toy is what belonged, once upon a time, to the economic and
the sacred, but no more.*

*It is no more the case that the soul of the toy is the cipher of history,
equipment for transforming conditions into diagnoses.*

[...] monster that surpasses all understanding.
Mourning nothing is the most difficult.

The beginning therefore is not authentic unless it contains, like a germ maturing, its own refutation, unless it is capable of itself producing this refutation, pulling it out of itself.

The hole at the summit undoes the beginning, it prohibits it from holding its own; from continuing and confirming itself in its own refutation. Where it was, NOTHING appears.

The horror of nothing to see [...],
[and not heard from a little plaything
the p"e.e.l.s.", tolls, and knells that replay
dad's *no-mos* barked and growled].

[Everything takes place as though in an empty room, the primal scene where one is present at one's own expense and so in no danger of getting lost.]

[And]
the child unlucky in [her] little State,
some hearth where freedom is excluded,
a hive whose honey is fear and worry.

A child who does not yet speak reacts differently to punishment than to brutality.

These ontological locales are fundamentally uninhabitable.

These are your riches, your great store; and yet
This is the use of memory:
For liberation—not less of love but expanding
Of love beyond desire
         mixing
Memory and desire—
Something like twilight, bluish and pinkish; a dream of
   voluptuous pleasure during an eclipse.
[Days without number:]
Between two waves of the sea.
Quick now, here, now, always—

Love is itself unmoving.
Speech without words
decay[s] with imprecision.
       Words strain,
Crack and sometimes break, under the burden,
Under the tension, slip, slide, perish
[...], will not stay in place,
Will not stay still.

Some of these poems first appeared in various forms in 6X6, *Aufgabe*, *The Brooklyn Rail*, *Denver Quarterly*, *Ink Node*, *Invisible Ear*, *mid)rib*, *Model Homes*, and *Skein*. "An Illusion of the Future" also appears in the chapbook *Just Kids*, published by Agnes Fox Press in 2012.

Many thanks to the following people for their help with this manuscript: Eric Baus, Marie Buck, Jamie Cooper, Brad Flis, Rob Fitterman, Josef Kaplan, David Need, Seth Parker, Adra Raine, Kim Rosenfield, Lauren Spohrer, Aaron Winslow, and Steve Zultanski. Thanks also to Matvei Yankelevich, who was supportive of the manuscript through its various manifestations and who provided much-needed feedback. This work would not have been possible without the offhand advice of Miriam Rodriguez all those years ago.

The author and publisher would like to acknowledge Abraham Adams, Alena Jones and Daniel Owen for their assistance with proofreading.

This book was made possible in part by a generous grant from the National Endowment for the Arts and with the support of the New York City Department of Cultural Affairs, in partnership with the City Council.

NATIONAL
ENDOWMENT
FOR THE ARTS

COLOPHON

This is the first edition of *Christian Name*.

The copyright is asserted by Lawrence Giffin as of 2012.

The edition is limited to 1,300 copies.

The ISBN is 978-1-933254-93-7, and the book is distributed to the trade by Small Press Distribution (www.spdbooks.org).

The artwork in this book and on the covers is by Lauren Pakradooni from her "Mirage Series" (2011).

The design of the book was accomplished by Don't Look Now! in collaboration with the author; typeset in Garamond and Didot.

The book was printed and bound in the United States by McNaughton & Gunn on FSC-certified recycled paper, with covers printed offset at Polyprint Design on paper from French Paper Co.

Ugly Duckling Presse
The Old American Can Factory
232 Third Street #E-303
Brooklyn, NY 11215

For a full catalog, please visit www.uglyducklingpresse.org.